Birding Through Life

Birding Through Life

Wanderings of a Born Birder

Allen H. Benton, Ph.D.

YBK Publishers, Inc. New York

Birding Through Life: Wanderings of a Born Birder

Copyright © 2004 by Allen H. Benton

All rights reserved including the right of reproduction in whole or in part in any form.

Photo credits: Front cover—Allen H. Benton;
    Back cover—Marjorie Benton

Design and typesetting: Noel Harrington, New York City

YBK Publishers, Inc.
425 Broome St.
New York, NY 10013

ISBN 0970392397

Library of Congress Control Number: 2004116103

Manufactured in the United States of America

Ver 4-12

To my wife, Marjorie, helpmeet at home, companion and bird-spotter in the field, my proof-reader and friendly critic, and always my best friend.

Sights like these when you're traveling blind
Through the brambles and devious trails
Make such an impact, so fix on the mind,
You'll never forget them till memory fails.

Ernest G. Tabor

CONTENTS

Preface

Many birders can (and will, in excruciating detail) recount the exact moment when they became aware of the seductive beauty and wonder of birds. Whether it be Roger Tory Peterson's tale of the dormant flicker, or an ordinary event like a chickadee landing on head or hand at a feeder, or simply an observation of an extraordinarily beautiful bird for the first time, this moment of epiphany is apparently a common experience.

I can claim no such epiphany. So far as I can remember, looking back over the memories of eighty years, I have always been an observer of avian life, entranced by the glint of sunlight on an iridescent head, the flash of a golden wing lining, the warble of the unseen bird in a treetop.

My earliest memories of birds are, inevitably, mere flashes: a brilliant male cardinal, unknown in our region at that time, perched briefly in a small tree in our front yard; a warbling vireo, though I didn't know what it was at the time, bubbling endlessly in the tall maples in our yard; the shining of black and yellow as a goldfinch bounced through the summer sky; the nest of a sparrow, probably a savannah sparrow, uncovered by accident during the aimless searching of a small boy.

My family, for generations on both sides, have been respectable but comparatively impoverished farmers. If there were any who had any leaning in the direction of bird study, they kept it well hidden. My mother enjoyed birds, but I think it may have been to large extent because it allowed her to share some moments with me, her youngest and often neglected son. Certainly she encouraged my interest, and shared it with me as much as a busy farm housewife could.

My first bird book, obtained when I was eight or ten years old, was the pocket-sized booklet by Chester A. Reed. I learned eventually that Reed had made a lot of mistakes—that his paintings were mostly poorly executed and often inaccurate; but the little book nourished my craving for knowledge of birds for years. The first Peterson field guide was still some years in the future, and the expensive illustrated books on birds were beyond our income.

A kindly state education department, however, had placed in each little country school a copy of the illustrations from E. H. Eaton's "Birds of New York,"—gorgeous paintings by Louis Agassiz Fuertes. I nearly read the print from the pages, and wished fervently for a copy of my own. It took twenty years for that dream to come to fruition. What I needed, more than anything else, was a catalyst to confirm and solidify my love of birds. One was finally provided when I was about twelve years old by the arrival in our small rural community of new neighbors.

The husband had been a successful and presumably well-to-do lawyer on the west coast. Rumor had it that he had become involved in some form of illegal activity and had been disbarred, but rumors are not necessarily fact.

Perhaps he was simply tired of the law, or of urban life, and having made enough money to allow him to retire, he had done so. In any case, he returned to his native countryside and bought an abandoned and rundown farm adjacent to that of his brother, who had remained on the family farm where he was born and where he remained.

Whatever the reason, his decision had a profound effect on me. His wife was an intelligent and talented woman who had had a responsible job until, crossing a street, she had been struck by a car. She was in critical condition for some time, and emerged with damaged hearing, no sense of smell whatever, and various other disabilities. She was apparently mentally sound, though perhaps psychologically damaged, but I was too young at the time to notice such things.

One thing she had not lost, in any case, was her interest in nature. She had an extensive library of nature books, and when she found out about my interest in nature, she was generous in sharing both her books and her knowledge. Among the many people who, in one way or another, have led me to the kind of life I have enjoyed, she was second only to my mother—second in a long line which included teachers, employers, contemporary friends, and even casual acquaintances.

One of the earliest photographs of me shows me, slightly out of focus, sitting on a crate in the yard with a fledged but flightless barn swallow perched quietly on my finger. This was clearly a harbinger of a life spent enjoying birds. Now that I can no longer get into the field, I have to enjoy in memory some of my thousands of great bird experiences, and I have selected a few of them that are particularly memorable to share with you in the following pages. I certainly hope you enjoy them, but whether you do or not, I will have had much enjoyment from reliving them.

I

A Connecticut Warbler
in the Cornfield

There are many brief flashes that come back to me of moments when I had a particularly close or exciting contact with a bird. I recall sitting in a sweet cherry-tree enjoying myself when a cedar waxwing, there on the same mission, perched no more than an arm's length away. Similarly, one day when I was high up in an Astrakhan apple tree (you may correctly deduce that I was an inveterate tree climber) a ruby-throated hummingbird landed a few feet away, regarded me for a moment, and then, as I sat absolutely still, flew to its tiny nest on a nearby branch and settled itself on its eggs. A much more unusual occurrence, one which I remember with absolutely clarity, involves a Connecticut warbler, a rare bird in central New York.

On a farm, the youngest boy gets a number of duties commensurate with his physical ability. He can do most jobs associated with dairy cows, and one of those daily duties, back in the 1930s when cows were pastured overnight as well as all day when the weather was warm enough, was to go to the pasture twice daily and bring the cows to the barn. In this I was usually assisted by a collie dog, so it was not a tough job, just something that had to be done, every day, twice a day.

In fact, this was one farm duty that I positively enjoyed. On the way to the pasture I could pause to pick a few cherries, or to watch a bird, or perhaps a weasel running along the stone wall, or whatever fragment of nature I chanced to see. In early autumn, I would often detour through a cornfield, where the stalks were much higher than my head, because migrating warblers and sparrows could often be seen picking insects from the corn.

I didn't always recognize the birds I saw, but sometimes there were birds that I could look up in the bird book when I was done with my chores. Thus it was that I saw, one memorable day, a bird that would have delighted a much more experienced birder than I almost anywhere in North America—a Connecticut warbler. I don't suppose that anyone ought to expect to see a Connecticut warbler in a cornfield, and I don't suppose that any committee which evaluated bird observations would accept this one. Probably I wouldn't do so myself if I were placed in that position. The bird is so rare that I have seen only one more in seventy years of birding, and that one was caught in a mist net by a friend who was a bird-bander.

I was on my way to the pasture one September evening, and seeing birds flying around in the corn I decided to take a detour. I turned into one of the rows and began to move slowly down the field. Most of the birds flew away as I approached, and while I could recognize an occasional yellow warbler or song sparrow, most of them eluded me.

Then, on a cornstalk only a few feet away, a small olive green and yellowish bird landed and just sat and looked at me. Its dark hooded head, its prominent white eye ring, its yellowish underparts, made it unmistakable. I don't know how long we stood looking at each other—probably only a few seconds—but it was long enough for me to fix in my memory every detail, and to be able to recognize the bird when I saw its picture in my book. Of its rarity, I learned many years later. Until I became a much more mature and experienced birder, I quite naturally did not see many rare birds. I didn't get out enough, I could not have recognized them if I had seen them unless they were particularly striking, and, then, rare birds are called that because they're seen only rarely even if you spend a lot of time looking for them. This gives me all the more reason to cherish that brief look at a once-in-a-lifetime bird.

And perhaps there is yet another reason. Peter Cashwell, in his book, *The Verb "to Bird"*, notes that the sightings from which he derives the most satisfaction are not necessarily the most beautiful or the most unusual birds, but the most unexpected. Possibly that explains the glow of satisfaction I get as I relive that moment when I met a Connecticut warbler in the cornfield—a bird that was both unexpected and rare, and unusually beautiful too.

II

A Comforting Goldfinch

In the progress of a long and for the most part happy life, birds have been a delight and joy, and on more than one occasion when life had taken a less happy turn, they have been a comfort as well. Among those times of mixed stress and joy, one particular day stands out in my memory.

One Fourth of July, when I was about twelve years old, my older brother and I were enjoying the meager stock of firecrackers that we could afford (a few small firecrackers and perhaps one or two torpedoes) when he complained of not feeling well. Only very sick people or emergency cases called for a doctor in those days and in our circumstances, but every farm housewife was prepared to handle minor incidents of illness or accident. My mother put my brother to bed, took his temperature, and from time to time checked on his progress. By that evening, he had broken out with the unmistakable blotches of measles.

We categorized measles as two types, which we called German or three-day measles, and black measles, or nine-day measles. This totally unscientific classification was based on the seriousness and duration of the diseases. Three-day measles (now known as rubellla) was no more than a minor inconvenience unless complications arose, though we now know that it can cause major damage to pregnant women, or more precisely to their offspring. Black measles, though, was a serious disease, which caused a high fever, night sweats, and a host of other symptoms, and which lasted nine or ten days. My brother, it soon became quite evident, had the latter variety. We were in for a long siege.

The progress of his case was normal, and in about ten days he was up and about. By that time, unfortunately, I was down with the disease, and our father, who had not had the disease in childhood, was beginning to show the symptoms too. Whereas my brother had suffered a rather mild case, my father and I were both very ill. We had alarmingly high fever, and our sheets had to be changed each day because they were drenched with sweat. My poor mother, trying to keep the farm work going during our busiest season, with only the help of my barely recovered brother, while caring for two very sick and demanding invalids, was frantic with care and worry. At last, as the illness ran its course, I began to feel well enough to want to do something. The rule in those days was to keep a measles sickroom dark, and my father was in the same room and not yet past the worst of his sickness, so I could not have a light to read by. However, my mother allowed me to turn around in my bed so my head was in front of the window, open the curtain enough so that I could see out, and raise the window a bit to let some fresh air into the hot stuffy room.

At last, I was able to look out over the lawn and garden, smell the fragrance of new-mown hay and the nearby rose garden, and perhaps see an occasional car pass on the road. Some ten yards away, my mother's clothesline ran across my field of vision, and to my delight a lovely male goldfinch, in the full glory of his black and yellow summer plumage, landed right in front of me. Then he began to warble the lovely twittery song that gave his species the name "wild canary." Looking, it seemed to me, directly at me as I peered from the window, he warbled on and on. It was as though he sang for me alone, and had chosen that spot to minister to the pain and loneliness of a sick child. Of course, I was old enough to know that this was not literally true. Somewhere within hearing distance, a female goldfinch was no doubt sitting on a small nest lined with thistledown, for goldfinches are among our latest nesters, and even now, though it was already nearly the first of August, they were still in the nesting stage. Still, for me that few moments of song, before the bird flew off with its bounding flight and its per-chic-o-ree call, was a blessed gift which has remained vivid in memory for seventy years.

III

Becoming an Ornithologist

In 1938, I graduated from high school, and because there was no employment to be had in those depression years, I took another year of high school to stave off the inevitable as long as possible. In June of 1939, with no chance of further education, I was forced to look about for some means of making a livelihood.

Making enough money to live on was a major challenge. I was lucky in having a place to live on the family farm, though it was obvious that they could not long support me unless I brought in some income. For the next nine months, I did whatever farm work I could find (I knew nothing else). The going rate was 10 cents per hour, or $1.00 a day if you worked a long day, and for that pittance I hoed corn, pitched hay, picked beans in summer and pulled beans in fall, worked on threshing gangs and silo filling gangs, picked hundreds of bushels of apples and helped to harvest acres of corn and beans. There was, if nothing else was available, always work at home, and even if I had a job I helped at home with morning and evening chores and whatever else I might be needed for. Of course, there was no money in working at home, and it was evident that something more was necessary.

In the spring of 1940, when I got home from a long day of working on a neighboring farm, my mother told me that the local teacher of agriculture had called and told me to come see him at my earliest convenience, as he had something to tell me that might be to my benefit—the understatement of the century, as it turned out. When I went to see him the next day, he told me that Sears Roebuck, the big mail-order company, was offering some scholarships to poor farm boys who had good academic records and wanted to study in a college of agriculture. Twenty of these scholarships had been allotted to Cornell's College of Agriculture, and he thought I might stand a chance of getting one. Although I had been out of school for a year, I had been valedictorian of my class of 19 students, majoring in agriculture in high school, and might thus be a good candidate.

With many misgivings, I applied, and in early summer received notice that I was one of the chosen. The scholarship provided me with the princely sum of $150: half upon my registration at Cornell, and the other half at the beginning of the second semester if my performance was satisfactory. I completed the necessary red tape to apply to Cornell and in August I was accepted into the College of Agriculture.

The only thing I knew about Cornell was that our teachers of agriculture had studied there, so I chose that as my major. In early September, with $5.00 in my pocket and considerable doubt in my mind, I went to Ithaca and began to wander the streets looking for work to keep body and soul together as I pursued my education.

Through the caring guidance of my advisor, Dr. John Hertel, I found an appropriate job, and Dr. Hertel, sensing that I had an interest in science, also told me that I had many options other than teaching agriculture. When he found my interests lay in nature, he arranged appointments for me with several professors in botany, ornithology, and other sciences.

Ornithology was headed up by Dr. Arthur A. Allen, a noted researcher but an even more noted teacher. As soon as I walked into Fernow Hall for my interview, and saw in his office a huge mounted emperor penguin which had been presented to him for his work connected with the South Polar explorations of Richard Byrd, I knew that I had found my intellectual home. In a short time I was enrolled as a major in ornithology and wildlife management, a dream come true for me.

Unlike most of my classmates, I knew nothing of scientific ornithology and was not even a skilled bird-watcher. I was starting from scratch, and it soon became evident that I was not going to contribute much to ornithology until I learned a great deal, the sooner the better.

My first contribution to ornithology was a very minor one, but an important one for me. I was employed at the home of Dr. Lawrence MacDaniels, chairman of the Floriculture program and a noted botanist. I helped with the housework, mowed the lawn in season, stoked the coal stove in winter, picked and graded apples in fall and pruned the trees in winter: in short, I did whatever was needed. Between chores, I was treated more or less as a member of the family, a privilege which I was careful not to abuse. The MacDaniels family maintained a bird feeder, visible from the living room window, and I spent a good deal of time watching it and learning to know all of the birds that appeared. One day, a bird came that none of us had ever seen before. Although I had by this time acquired a copy of the first edition of Peterson's field guide, I could not find this bird anywhere in it.

At the student center, there was a considerable library which included some books of special interest, and there one night I came upon W. E. Clyde Todd's *Birds of Western Pennsylvania*, illustrated by one of the Cornell professors, George Sutton. Leafing through the illustrations, I came upon a perfect rendering of the bird I had been seeing—an immature white-crowned sparrow. I announced my discovery proudly to the MacDaniels family and to my fellow students, and since this was a comparatively rare winter bird quite a few of the latter wanted to come and see it.

Among them was Harold Axtell, an older student who had had a career as a musician but had given it up at the age of 35 and returned to college to become an ornithologist. He was a consummate field birder, and over the next few years taught me a great deal, and in this case he was the first to note that the bird I was seeing had a small dark line from eye to beak which marked it as the western race of white-crowned sparrow, then known as Gambel's sparrow. A major discovery! No Gambel's sparrow had ever been seen in Ithaca.

Some of the ornithologists, of course, wanted to collect the bird and put its skin in the museum, but the MacDanielses said "No way." They did, however, consent to having it live-trapped so it could be examined, photographed and properly documented. Under my direction, the trap was set in a spot which the bird often frequented, and it was obliging enough to walk in promptly, whereupon I delivered it, trap and all, to the curator of the museum, Bill Montagna, so he could compare it with skins in the museum.

As I stood by, Bill carefully removed the bird from the trap and studied its face carefully. Then he wet a finger and rubbed the dark area. It disappeared! Instead of a Gambel's sparrow, we had a white-crown with a dirty face! It was an anti-climax. Of course Harold Axtell was mortified, and I was for a day or two a minor departmental celebrity—a status which I had not previously enjoyed. It was a heady experience, and the true beginning of my lifelong career as a birder.

IV

My First Century Run

O f all the many arcane and weird rituals indulged in by birders, none is more strange than the "century run." At the peak of the spring migration, which is, in the northeast, around the middle of May, a group of birders will attempt to record sightings of more than one hundred species of birds in a single day. Some strict conservatives insist that each bird must be seen and identified by at least two members of the group in order to be counted. Others will accept a bird which is seen by one member but flies away before anyone else can see it, or will accept records based on sound only. This makes it easier to find an owl, which is easy to hear but hard to see in the dark, and also to record birds during the dawn chorus even though they are not visible. Such elusive but noisy singers as the white-eyed vireo can thus be recorded by voice alone, if the song or call is sufficiently distinctive to make it impossible to mistake it.

Technically, the period of the century run is from midnight to midnight, but most birders will settle for a 3 a.m. or 4 a.m. start, and a final tally at around nine or ten at night. Of course, when different teams are contesting for the greatest count, they may choose to use the whole twenty-four hours, in the hope of out-counting their competitors. A 3 a.m. start, however, gives ample time to record several owls, and to then hear the dawn chorus at its fullest. In the evening, the night flight of the woodcock or the ovenbird can be recorded as soon as it is dark, which will certainly have occurred by 10 p.m.

If you are the typical non-birder, or even a beginning birder, the idea of seeing or hearing a hundred species in one day may seem an impossible goal. You probably don't even know a hundred birds, including those that you see only in winter at your feeders. Actually, the record number is much higher than 100; at last report, it was about 230 species. There are a number of mind-numbing century runs like the Montezuma Muck Race in central New York and the World Series of Birding along the Atlantic coast in New Jersey and adjacent areas, when several teams vie for prizes and would consider a mere hundred species an abject failure.

In theory, I should have participated in my first century run in 1941, when I was a freshman and was taking the beginning ornithology course. However, during that year I was working about 35 hours a week, and much of that time was of necessity on Sunday, so I had to pass up on the century run that year. In 1942, I was living near campus and working fewer hours, so it was possible for me to join the group. It occurred on May 16, and I was a member of a group consisting of Harold Axtell, who figures prominently in a later chapter, his wife, Rachel, also an accomplished birder, Herbert Bleich, Norman Levardsen, also freshmen, and me, the least knowledgeable and possibly most eager of the group.

Both Norm and I hoped that some of Harold's birding expertise would rub off on us before the day ended.

In the standard mode, we assembled at the chilly pre-dawn hour of 3:00 a.m. Our first stop was at a known screech owl territory, where Harold was able to whistle up our first bird of the day. (Screech owls do not screech. They whistle, in an eerie sort of way; they bark like a small dog; but they don't screech. Nor do they hoot.) Encouraged by our first success, we drove to a wooded valley some miles away where, by 4:00 a.m., the first voices of the dawn chorus were beginning to be heard. We sorted out the song sparrows, various thrushes and warblers, and by 5:00 a.m. we had a goodly list. This was followed by a futile search for an upland sandpiper, which managed to escape visual identification, but which made our list (Harold's, at least) because his very sensitive ears detected its distant song, which the rest of us couldn't hear.

I will not bore you with a full account of the day's activities, which covered some two hundred miles of driving and eighteen or nineteen of the twenty-four hours allotted. From Ithaca, we drove north along the east shore of Cayuga Lake to a state preserve called Howland's Island, then to the Montezuma National Wildlife Refuge, and back down the west side of the lake to Ithaca. I was not keeping a life list at that time, so I can't tell you how many birds I saw or heard for the first time, but there were many. My personal list was 116 species, and I'm sure Harold's was a good bit more.

Among my memories of that day, one of the most vivid was of a bird I didn't see. Along toward evening, we stopped beside a wet field where, Harold had been told, a sedge wren, then called the short-billed marsh wren, might be heard. We pulled off beside the road and parked, and from somewhere off in the field came an undistinguished series of chirps and chatters which Harold assured us was the desired species. We all dutifully checked it off on our lists, but it was many years before I could honestly place it on my life list. From time to time I heard one again, but I was nearly eighty years old before I actually saw one well enough to identify it without being told what it was. That occurred when a colony of several pairs was found in two adjacent fields only a couple of miles from my home.

It was after ten p.m. when Harold dropped me off at my rooming house, exhausted but happy after my first experience with that particular rite of passage. Six months later, I would be in the Army and off to the war, and it was five years before I could participate in another century run: one in which Harold Axtell also participated, but which is the subject of another chapter.

V

High Spots on the High Peaks

After two years at Cornell, I had made the first few hesitant steps toward becoming a professional naturalist. My frequent field trips with Harold Axtell and my obvious eagerness to pick his brain led to my first employment in a more or less professional capacity as the director of nature study at the Lake Placid Club in the Adirondack village of the same name.

The Lake Placid Club, now defunct, was for most of a century a refuge for the rich, the powerful, the white and the non-Jewish. (They may have barred other groups as well, for all I know.) Founded by the Dewey family, one of whom originated the Dewey Decimal System of library arrangement as well as the Dewey Simplified Spelling System, it catered to kings, presidents, industrialists, and those with that kind of money and the right background. For some years, Harold had served as director of their nature activities, leading field trips around the central Adirondacks. In

1942, having reached the age of 40 or thereabouts, Harold was anxious to complete his doctorate and get a paying job. No doubt Rachel, his patient wife, was also ready to be relieved of the responsibility of supporting them, though I never heard her complain. In any case, a replacement for the Lake Placid job was needed, and Harold was asked to recommend someone. I was never quite sure why he chose me, but I suspect that he was scraping the bottom of the barrel. I was a long way from his level of expertise and had no experience in the Adirondacks. I also had no experience in teaching at any level, while this job would require teaching everyone from small children to old people. But Harold, knowing that I was a fast learner and needed summer work, recommended me for the job, and I was hired.

The club, I found when I arrived there near the end of June of 1942, was about as far from my experience in life as one could imagine. Used to living among hard-scrabble farmers all my life, I found myself chatting with wealthy gentlemen like Mr. Doehler, founder of Doehler Die Company, who tried (unsuccessfully) to teach me to play chess; Westbrook van Voorhies, the voice of The March of Time, one of the most popular radio news programs of the 1940s—or more accurately with his wife and daughter, both of whom had some interest in nature; a Mr. Howe, descendant of the inventor of the sewing machine, who calling me aside one day, said, "I think young men like you ought to be encouraged," and handed me a ten-dollar bill. Since I was getting about that amount for a week's work, it was quite a boost to my finances. King Peter of Yugoslavia was there, though not really a king any more, since he had been driven out by Marshal Tito. He was accompanied by several dangerous-looking bodyguards, and did not mingle much with the other guests. My only contact with him was when he attended the theater one might and I was chosen to escort him and his entourage, quite discreetly and in complete darkness, to their seats.

This only hints at the diversity of my duties. I was one of a group of college students known as G-boys. Since I was single and unattached, I was pressed into service with them, something that Harold had not done and had not warned me about. The G stood for gigolo, because a major part of our duties was to squire young ladies around whenever we were not actively engaged in other duties. Since they were all rich, mostly quite lovely and quite intelligent, this was a pleasant duty. Another assignment was involved with classical music, which I found equally pleasant. A group of musicians from the Eastman-Rochester music school were employed for the summer, and since they played at different places around the club grounds, it was necessary to have someone carry their stand and music and the less fragile instruments from place to place. That job fell to the G-boys, and I volunteered to work the weekly chamber music concerts, which allowed me to enjoy a lot of good music while discharging my duties. Still another duty was physically more demanding but equally enjoyable. The club sponsored a hiking club and in view of my presumed expertise in the out-of-doors, I was appointed their leader and chaperon. Since I was little or no older than most of them, it seemed a bit silly to think of me as their chaperon, but it was fun and it allowed me to get a look at the birds and the plants of areas not reachable in my regular nature walks.

To better prepare me for those walks, Harold had provided long lists of both birds and plants, along with specific directions as to where I might find them. Following his instructions, I was able to lead reasonably productive field trips, although the number of participants was quite small, usually little more than a half dozen. I also gave periodic talks (but not field trips) to the children's group. This led to an interesting discovery.

One of the employees who became a fast friend was the female tennis professional, Madame Sylvia Henrotin, who gave me a few free tennis lessons and also shared any information which she thought might be of help to me. One day, while working with the children, Mme. Henrotin noticed an odd cabinet in a corner. Opening it, she found that it contained a small collection of stuffed birds, and these became one of the mainstays of my teaching, both with the children and with my weekly lectures to the adults.

Lake Placid is in the center of the High Peaks area of the Adirondacks. The three highest mountains, Marcy, McIntyre and Whiteface, were all within a few miles and we hiked to all of them. At their higher elevations I saw and heard Swainson's and gray-cheeked thrushes, yellow-bellied flycatchers, boreal chickadees and other birds which were new to me or previously seen only as passing migrants in central New York. Now I could hear them, watch them and really get to know them.

In those golden days of youth among the rich and privileged, where I was accepted as one of them despite my background of poverty, it is hard to select single incidents as more memorable than others, but one was different enough to remain vividly in my memory. The Adirondack Mountain Club, which developed and maintained trails in the area, was interested in developing a trail along the then uncharted ridge of the Sentinel Range so they asked the Hiking Club to map a possible route. It was entirely bushwhacking through a region completely devoid of trails, navigating by compass, and only a few hardy souls volunteered. Sam Packer, de facto chairman of the group, I as its nominal leader, and two young ladies made up our expeditionary group. One of the girls was only fourteen years old but game for anything. The other was a part-time model who had recently appeared on the cover of Life Magazine, but didn't complain about getting scratched, dirty and bruised in places during the long hike.

For me, the difficulties of the hike were made less troublesome by a small group of boreal chickadees, who accompanied us along the ridge and querulously questioned our presence with a constant stream of "chee-day-day" and other chirping calls.

Having traversed the assigned route, we turned to the left and fought our way through the brush to the Lake Placid-Wilmington highway, where we were to meet our chauffeur. After hours of blind hiking through uncharted wilderness, we hoped we would not have to travel too far along the road to reach the car, but Sam's navigational skills had proved equal to the situation. As we emerged from the dense wilderness and tried to decide which way to go to look for the car, it appeared on our right. Our patient chauffeur soon had us comfortably and safely on our way home.

From the birding point of view, the summer was satisfactory, to me at least, and I think to my nature-loving friends. My Adirondack bird list for the summer was precisely 100 bird species, and included lots of red crossbills, Lincoln's sparrow, peregrine falcon, olive-sided and yellow-bellied flycatchers, and one rare black-backed woodpecker, the subject of the next chapter.

Near the end of that summer, I was called to take my draft physical. The next step, quite predictably, was that in a very short time I would be a private in some branch of Uncle Sam's military, a far cry from that last luxurious summer of freedom and pleasure.

VI

Of Woodpeckers and Politicians

In general, my life has been singularly free from contacts with major political figures (or even minor ones, for that matter.) During my thirteen years in Albany, when I taught at the State University, I had several occasions to meet with the Mayor, the legendary Erastus Corning III, but I have never meddled much in politics, and politicians have seldom meddled with me.

One of the few exceptions to this occurred during the summer of 1942 at the Lake Placid club. The politician was the Honorable Thomas C. Desmond, State Senator from Newburgh and one of the most powerful figures in New York politics at that time. Senator Desmond suffered from an allergy to ragweed, so during the late summer he usually took refuge in some place where that noxious weed did not flourish. In New York, that meant the highest place he could find, and this led him to the central Adirondacks, and since he was sufficiently rich and distinguished, to the Lake Placid Club.

The senator was an austere and forbidding figure, and I would normally have had no contact with him, but it happened that he was also something of a bird-watcher. When he found out that there was a nature counselor who was also a bird-watcher, he sought me out and asked if I would take him to some places where we might find interesting and unusual birds. He had a car and enough gasoline coupons to run it, so my choices were not restricted to my usual field trip locations.

Because of the senator's allergy, we had to stay away from fields and agricultural areas, of which there were few anyway. Further, his age and physical condition ruled out any efforts to study the mountaintop birds, which I had found so interesting. Our first trip was not terribly eventful, but we got to know each other and I learned that he had never seen the black-backed woodpecker (in those days known as the Arctic three-toed woodpecker). Harold Axtell had given me directions to a place known as the Chubb River Swamp, where this bird occurred, so I suggested to Senator Desmond that we try that, if he was willing to try a little swamp-hiking.

I had never seen the place, so I had little idea what we would be getting into. On one summer morning I had attempted to bicycle to the swamp, but had made a wrong turn somewhere and got lost. However, with Harold's directions in my hand and the senator to drive, we made it with no difficulty and parked at the edge of the bridge over the small river.

The Chubb River is a tributary of the Ausable River, and the swampy area through which it runs was, according to Harold's directions, the home of gray jays, spruce grouse, boreal chickadees and both species of three-toed woodpeckers. It seemed to me that we stood a good chance of seeing at least one or two of these rare and interesting birds.

With me, ignorant but undaunted, in the lead, we plunged into the forest. This would make a more interesting story if we had fallen into a bog, or got lost, or had some other misfortune, but in fact our trip was quite uneventful. The forest floor was moist, but it had been a fairly dry summer and we encountered no standing water. We strolled along easily until, a few hundred feet from the road, we discovered, or were discovered by, some boreal chickadees, the first of our desired species.

After a few satisfying moments of watching these little birds, we pressed farther into the swamp until we heard a delicate tapping which indicated some sort of woodpecker. Fortunately it was easy to find, and not particularly skittish, and we had the second of our wanted species—the black-backed woodpecker.

The senator and I were both pretty well satisfied, and although our further search for a gray jay or a spruce grouse was unsuccessful, we felt that our expedition had been worthwhile. A day or two later, the senator went back to either Albany or Newburgh, where I am sure he regaled his friends with the tale of his morning in a remote and untracked Adirondack swamp.

I have seen the black-backed woodpecker only once since that day—in a beaver swamp in northern Minnesota some 30 years later, when I was teaching at the University of Minnesota's summer program at Lake Itasca.

As for Senator Desmond, our paths never crossed again, since I was soon in the Army; when I got to Albany in 1949 he was either retired or soon to be so. I have always been grateful to him, though, for giving me the chance to see a new bird in a place which I would otherwise never have reached.

VII

I Begin Birding around the World

My transition from embryonic ornithologist to combat soldier began on October 1, 1942, when I was inducted into the Army at Syracuse. The Army kindly allowed us a two-week period to finish up whatever loose ends we might have (I used mine in a quick trip to New York City to visit some of my new friends from the Lake Placid Club) and on October 15 I was bussed to Fort Niagara for preliminary indoctrination, issuance of clothing and gear, shots against several diseases and other orientation. I was there only three days, and on October 18 was placed on a train, with no idea where I was going, and headed westward.

Our destination, we eventually found out, was Fort Riley, Kansas, and the Cavalry Replacement Training Center. According to a sign near the middle of this vast post, I was now exactly halfway across the United States. Before that, I had not been much more than 300 miles from home, and on only one or two occasions out of the state of New York, so my situation was new to me in more ways than one.

I had left home with nothing much more than the clothing I was wearing, knowing that the Army would supply the rest. Even though the exigencies of basic training allowed me little free time, I soon asked my parents to send my binoculars, hoping I could get some opportunities to see a few of the unfamiliar birds in my new environment. Occasionally, on a free Sunday afternoon, I would walk down to the Republican River, which ran along the post only a few hundred yards from my barracks. Here I added to my life list such birds as the tufted titmouse, red-bellied woodpecker, lazuli bunting, Harris' sparrow and a few others.

After three weeks of introductory training, testing and such, the Army, in what we came to regard as typical Army fashion, assigned me to truck-driving school. Since I could not drive, had never had a license, and had certainly never come close to driving a truck, this probably made some kind of Army sense, though I couldn't figure it out. I found out, however, that truck driving had some advantages. Our training consisted largely of road marches to various places within fifty or sixty miles of the post, and often these were good places to watch birds. We usually had a lunch break at some park or other area where a lot of vehicles could find parking space, and those places made it possible for me to do a little birding.

The list of the birds I saw at Fort Riley was an extensive one, and included a pair of cinnamon teal along the river bank, a scissor-tailed flycatcher perched on a fence, a LeConte's sparrow, encountered on one of the field exercises characterized as "creeping and crawling," a large variety of shore birds on a lunch stop at Herington Lake, and many more memorable species. After my basic training I was selected for Officer Candidate School, and remained at

Fort Riley while the rest of my group went on to an uncertain future somewhere else.

After a few months, when I had already been accepted for a session of OCS, my first sergeant, perhaps sensing a little ambivalence or perhaps just convinced that I would not be a very good officer, asked me if I would rather stay in the troop as a non-com. I agreed, and for the next year as a non-com I had more time and opportunity for birding.

Another corporal and I were assigned in June of 1943 to take some fifty soldiers to the Desert Training Center in Hyder, Arizona, with a three-day delay en-route on the way back. This allowed me to spend a couple of days poking around Phoenix, and though it was blazing hot and the only place for birding was a city park, I found a couple of good birds: My life list was enriched with the pyrrholoxia and the black-throated sparrow. From my seat on the train I picked up some burrowing owls, a Gila woodpecker, and a few others.

Fort Riley was just on the edge of the area covered by Peterson's field guide, so when the western guide came out a Cornell friend, Rudd Stone, sent me a copy. This allowed me to identify a Cassin's sparrow, whose mating flight and almost complete lack of field marks made it easy when I had the right book, but impossible otherwise. The book's real value, however, came a little later when, in March of 1944, I was transferred to Camp Hood, Texas, made an infantryman, and then sent to Fort Ord, California, en route to a combat assignment overseas.

VIII

Stalking the White-eyed Vireo

Camp Hood, now known as Fort Hood and a huge operation, was at that time a sprawling camp divided into two sections covering some hundred or so square miles west of Temple. North Camp was occupied by the tank destroyer school, while South Camp, where I was located, housed a brand new Infantry Replacement Training Center.

Here in Texas I was in the midst of a fascinating avifauna, made up of southern, eastern and western species. Sadly, I never had the opportunity or the knowledge to observe its two most interesting species, the black-capped vireo and the golden-cheeked warbler, species which have now been responsible for the development of a major ornithological study station right there at Fort Hood.

My biggest bird day in Texas, though, is not hard to select. I had been there only a couple of weeks when I got a weekend pass, and went to Austin, some sixty miles or so to the south. On Sunday morning I was up early and off for a day of birding.

The Colorado River passes through Austin, and at one point a large bend had been dammed to create a long narrow lake called, in a fit of originality, Lake Austin. On the side away from the city, the cedar-clad hills and deep gullies were completely wild and uninhabited, and I decided to go there. I rented a rowboat, made my way across the lake, and climbed up to the top of the first hill.

As I reached the top, I heard among the dense cedars a very distinctive song, one which I had never heard before. I approached cautiously, only to hear the song farther away. When I continued to follow it, it flew back over my head and continued to sing behind me. The sneaky bird led me a merry chase over that hilltop for a half hour or so, during which time I never caught sight of it, so I gave up the unequal contest and continued on my way.

It was a long time before I heard that song again, but in the meantime I had found out that it was a white-eyed vireo. On the rare occasions when I hear it now, I am carried back to those dense cedars, through which I crawled, sweating and calling the elusive bird all kinds of names (but not its real one). The "chip-per-wee-chip" is not one of my favorite songs.

I proceeded to wander around the hilltop, and found that whichever way I went I encountered a steep cliff, down which I was evidently going to have to climb if I wanted to get down to the lake without retracing my footsteps. As I hung there on the cliff I heard another unfamiliar song, loud and ringing, echoing from the walls of the canyon like the nearby waterfalls, and I was afraid I was going to be in for another frustrating search. This one, however, proved less elusive and more cooperative and I was soon looking at the lovely reddish body and white throat of a canyon wren—properly named, it would appear, since I found it while crawling down the face of a canyon wall.

The summer passed quickly, with frequent encounters with such strange creatures as armadillos, roadrunners and a variety of reptiles. Before I was transferred to Fort Ord in September I had added to my life list Bell's vireo, a charming little bird somewhat easier to see than the white-eyed, the lesser goldfinch, Bewick's wren, a beautiful blue grosbeak, and at almost the same time the even more beautiful painted bunting, the golden-fronted woodpecker, black-chinned hummingbird, and a few others.

All too soon, the Army decided that I had spent enough time knocking around the United States and it was time for me to get down to the business of war. I left Camp Hood in the middle of a September night and headed westward for Fort Ord, the jumping-off point for the Pacific war.

IX

A Brief Stop in California

It has been sixty years since I left Fort Ord, and no doubt it has changed, since it was abandoned by the Army some years ago. In 1944, though, there were few places where you could see a greater variety of birds. The base fronted on the Pacific Ocean, and on a low bluff overlooking the ocean the Army had built a Service Club—quite possibly the most beautifully located Service Club in the country.

The base itself was largely Mediterranean habitat—oaks, mostly small; shrubby growth of chapparal and I don't know what other densely packed vegetation; patches of at least rudimentary forest. Each of these segments of my new environment had its characteristic birds. It was literally a birder's paradise, which, sadly, I was in no position to do much about.

October and November are, in any case, not the best months for birding, and those are the two months that I chanced to be in Fort Ord. Nevertheless, even allowing for the fact that my observations were made in a few minutes stolen away from other duties, and one memorable pass which allowed me to get a few miles away, I managed to add more birds to my life list there than I had in either Texas or Kansas.

My experience with oceanic birds had been exactly nil; I had never seen an ocean before. Of the hundreds of birds I saw from the bluff behind the Service Club, or from the beach below, I could identify only an occasional one. Three easily identified gulls, western, Heerman's and California; one shearwater, the commonest of all, the sooty; Pacific loon, white pelican, western grebe, Brandt's and pelagic cormorants, white-winged and surf scoters.

Inland, in the scrubby growth where we conducted our daily field exercises, were hundreds of tiny bush tits; in the oaks, acorn woodpeckers; both black and Say's phoebes; yellow-billed magpies; on one occasion, a merlin perched on a small tree, favoring with me a perfect view.

Most of the time, soldiers who were on their way overseas were not allowed off the post for more than an occasional evening. I was fortunate enough to be assigned a job escorting incoming soldiers to whatever kind of briefing or de-briefing they needed. This meant that I was on duty 24 hours every day, but it also meant that I was relieved from the onerous and unnecessary training, which I had already repeated seven times as cadre in two replacement centers. This duty also gave me the privilege of leaving the post on a couple of occasions, one of them my most memorable day of those two months in California.

What I needed most of all was a knowledgeable local birder, who could have helped me with identifications and told me of places to go, but I had no such person. Faced with an area I knew nothing about, and a vast array of birds I had never seen before, I was somewhat frustrated. On this day of freedom, I decided that I would go to Carmel, where I had been on one occasion at a USO dance, and then walk and hitch-hike around the Seventeen Mile Drive, which traverses the perimeter of the Monterey Peninsula.

Seventeen miles is a long way to walk in one day, and rides were scarce in those wartime days of gasoline shortages, but I managed to make the tour and see a few birds. I added golden-crowned sparrows, a black oyster-catcher, an avocet, Anna's hummingbird and a winter wren; not an impressive list, but a wonderful day away from the Army duties and the specter of imminent departure for parts unknown.

I arrived back at the base tired but happy. In the space of a week, with a short pass and a lot of luck, I had added twelve life birds to my list. It was near the end of my stay there, however. I left Fort Ord on November 19, and shortly after Thanksgiving, with several hundred other soldiers, I sailed out of San Francisco on a little Dutch-owned banana boat from the South Pacific trade. I was on my way to the war against the Japanese.

Some 35 years later I was able to return to Monterey, and with more time, greater knowledge, a more favorable time of year and a little luck, I added many of the species I had missed in 1944. In the meantime, I watched birds from California to New Guinea to Luzon to Honshu—a long and perilous journey made bearable only by an interest in the nature observed along the way.

X

Birding on the High Seas

When we left California, early in the afternoon of November 27, we had no idea where we were going. It was the Army's confident belief that if you didn't know, you couldn't tell anyone, so secrecy was the order of the day. Our transport was not particularly comfortable, since the holds previously used for the storage of various materials had just been cleared and fitted with bunks. The odor of some previous contents pervaded our sleeping space, and there was no way to avoid it. Our ship was large enough to hold a few hundred men, crammed in as close as possible, and except for the replacements, it contained a small contingent of anti-aircraft personnel, who would quite certainly have been useless in the face of a real air attack. We were alone and unescorted, so we had no defense whatever against submarine attack. Our hope of survival depended on the experience, skill and knowledge of the ship's captain, a grizzled

Dutchman who certainly knew the South Pacific well, though probably not the territory we would cover in the first couple of weeks of the voyage.

The trip was, however, quite uneventful, except for my seasickness, which lasted for three days, and no doubt caused me to lose a good bit of weight, something I didn't need. After I recovered, I spent as much of my time as possible on deck, where the fresh sea air seemed to help avert further nausea. In daylight I scanned the ocean for birds, but discovered only two species of albatross, which were always following the vessel in the hope of getting some food when the garbage was dumped. On one memorable day in mid-Pacific, a red-tailed tropic bird landed on the mast. I was probably the only passenger who noticed it, but I thoroughly enjoyed its brief visit. As we approached the South Pacific islands, we saw an occasional group of small white terns, which I presume were the ubiquitous fairy tern of that part of the world. Those few species were my return for endless hours of watching.

After almost four weeks of traveling with no idea of where we were bound, we at last sighted land. Our captain announced that we were passing through between Bougainville and Guadalcanal in the Solomon Islands, and would soon reach New Guinea. This more or less scotched any hope that we might be bound for Australia, since the big replacement depot for the Pacific war had been recently established on New Guinea near Lae.

Because of a case or two of mumps on board, we could not be landed there, so on Christmas eve we were unloaded in the beautiful harbor of Finschafen, a hundred or so miles up the coast. This was a sort of holding area, where we would stay until there was no danger of introducing mumps into the big replacement center. In the dusk of evening, we were quickly transferred to trucks and taken to a remote part of the base, where we were given bedding and a mosquito bar, and assigned to squad tents. Shortly thereafter the tropical darkness descended, and we crawled into our unfamiliar mosquito bar-protected beds and went to sleep.

XI

An Unexpected Meeting

At sunrise on Christmas morning, I was roused from slumber by loud raucous calls, somewhat crow-like in nature, though I'm sure their makers were not even distantly related to crows. Despite the fact that it was not time to get up and about, I could not resist the chance to see some new birds, so I quickly dressed and walked out in front of the tent. The noisy birds were, so far as I could detect, all black and somewhat larger than a grackle. As near as I could determine when I later got a New Guinea bird book, they were perhaps some species of honey-eater, or possibly related to birds-of-paradise. I did not study them very long, but walked down to the edge of a small stream which flowed by just a few yards from our tent. The scene was right from a Hollywood movie of a tropical paradise. Huge butterflies and colorful parakeets flew through the palm trees. Strange new birds flew high overhead, as well as along the stream and in the trees. If I had known what I was seeing, it would have been paradise for me, but all I could do was to write down a brief description, make a rough sketch, and hope that I would some day be able to discover what they were.

Some were easily placed in a family. A large copper-colored hawk that glided over the forest was so distinctive that I was eventually able to place it as the New Guinea version of the widespread Brahminy kite. Small bright blue kingfishers were also easy to place in a family, and small swifts overhead were also easily identified. Others were of families which I had never heard of, like a tiny flowerpecker and the black birds that had awakened me. It was great fun, but also immensely frustrating. Our life in Finschafen was nearly as idyllic as the setting. From time to time we were given labor duties, which we shirked industriously, but most of our time was our own, and I took full advantage of it to become acquainted with hermit crabs, a small flying squirrel-like mammal of the type known as a sugar glider, giant white cockatoos and small green parakeets, and all manner of other interesting fauna. Our idyllic life, unfortunately, lasted only about three weeks. We were to be transferred to the replacement depot, since no new cases of mumps had appeared, and from there we would be on our way to the combat zone a few thousand miles to the north.

We left Finschafen at night for the short run down the coast to Lae on a small ship that was not designed to transport people, so there was no place for us to sleep. We were just told to stay on deck, so we sat around on the unyielding steel plates and eventually stretched out and tried to sleep. Just before dawn, we anchored a few hundred yards offshore, and after daybreak we crawled down rope ladders to the waiting LCIs below. For the uninitiated, LCI stands for Landing Craft Infantry, but to those who had to use them and ride in them the initials stood for Lousy Civilian Invention.

The replacement depot was a huge tent city on a flat dry plain, with scarcely a tree in sight—a complete contrast to Finschafen's jungle situation. Our regimen was also completely different—every day we had one of two activities: either a long hike in the sweltering heat and humidity; or fatigue duty, usually digging the classic-eight-by-eight-by-eight holes for garbage disposal. I preferred the latter, because as a sergeant I didn't dig, I just supervised, which meant standing or sitting around and watching the birds. Of course I didn't see many; the most spectacular was a giant gallinule known as a purple swamp hen, much like the purple gallinule of our southern states but about twice the size.

After this kind of activity all day, we needed a bath, but our bath arrangements were exceedingly primitive. On a framework of poles, a steel drum was mounted and filled with water. After being heated by the sun all day, the water was pleasantly warm, and one could stand under it, pull on a rope, and release some water for a quick shower. One afternoon on my way to the bath I stopped to admire a willie wagtail, a small black and white bird quite appropriately named by the Australians. While I stood there, another soldier appeared, evidently also on the way to the bath, and much to my surprise he paused and said "Are you interested in birds?" In what had by now become nearly two and a half years in the Army, no one had ever asked me that. After the shock had abated I introduced myself and told him that yes, I was in civilian life an ornithology student at Cornell, and hoped to become an ornithologist after the war.

The interested stranger, it developed, was Tom Gilliard, an employee of the American Museum of Natural History in New York. After our brief latrine missions were completed, we went back to his tent and talked until Taps. He knew or knew of most of the people I knew in the field of ornithology, including some of the students, so we had a pleasant evening bringing each other up to date on the whereabouts of various mutual acquaintances. I met him soon again on the ship which carried us up to Luzon, and again, several years after the war, when the American Ornithologists' Union was meeting in New York. Attending the meeting, I took advantage of the opportunity to look in on him, and he showed me around his working area, and introduced me to Ernst Mayr, one of the authors of the book I had used in the Pacific.

After the war, Tom returned to the South Pacific and eventually became a leading authority on the birds of that part of the world. Sadly, while acquiring a vast knowledge of South Pacific bird life, Tom also acquired a disease of some sort—I never knew precisely what it was—and died while only in his fifties. While we were not close friends, of course, I treasured our brief acquaintance, and the very welcome break of meeting a fellow bird student amid the boredom of life at the replacement depot.

The bird life of the Lae area, what little I had the opportunity to see, was quite different from that at Finschafen. I saw a few common ones, like the pied triller and the aforementioned willie wagtail, but for the most part my time was taken up with non-ornithological pursuits.

We stayed at Lae about three weeks, during which Irving Berlin visited the post with his USO shows. He was already quite old, but his troupe was young and energetic. My seat for watching the show was several hundred yards from the stage on an Army truck's hood, so I didn't see him very well. Still, it was a nice change and I presume the show was good, though it was certainly not memorable.

Although we knew that the next stop for most of us would be a combat unit on Luzon, we were nonetheless deliriously happy when, about the first of February, we were called out for a roll call and most of us who had come overseas together were told to pack up and prepare to move out. We were on the way to the Philippines and the war.

Our last day on New Guinea was typically hectic. We were each issued a new carbine as a weapon, a lot of new clothing, new packs of the latest army model, and some clothing. The carbine and packs would be ditched as soon as we arrived in combat in favor of an M-1 rifle and a jungle pack, but of course we were ignorant of that, so we boarded our trucks and headed for the pier in good spirits, looking forward to the next step in our changing military careers.

XII

Combat Birding in Luzon

Our trip from New Guinea to Luzon was on an Australian vessel, with a small complement of British Marines as gunners if needed. This time we were part of a large convoy, including destroyers which rode on our flanks to protect us against submarine attack. The voyage was comparatively dull, enlivened occasionally by rough seas and once when the destroyers dropped depth charges, presumably having detected a submarine below. We had no duties, so we lay around on top of a stack of life rafts (we thought it would be good to be close to them if we needed them), read, talked and slept.

We landed at Lingayen Gulf about a month after the original assault at that point, and after a couple of days at the new replacement depot there, a group of some twenty of us were assigned to the 112th Cavalry Regimental Combat Team. We arrived at the regimental headquarters near the front lines north of Manila at about 4 a.m., and by noon we were assigned and delivered to front line troops, ready for our first taste of the real war.

For the next five months, I was on the front lines constantly, except for a few days when I was in the hospital for treatment of pinworms. The regiment was an independent unit, which was used for reconnaissance and as a guard of the flanks of the divisions fighting in the mountains. We spent four days in an assault on part of the Japanese lines, but most of the time we were patrolling into and behind the Japanese outpost line.

Such activities, of course, gave me little opportunity for birding, but I made the most of such opportunities as I had. At some point during my stay there, my copy of *Bird Life of the South Pacific*, by Mayr and DeSchaunsee , finally caught up with me after following me for several months. At last I was able to identify some of the birds I had seen in New Guinea, and some of the more widespread species I saw in Luzon.

As a counter-reconnaissance unit, we spent the day when we were not actively patrolling in watching the Japanese across the valley. Perched on the side of a hill, and armed with excellent binoculars, we could look across and watch for troop movements, unusual activity, and such. The binoculars, however, could be turned to watch any bird I might see, and in this way I identified the olive-colored sunbird, singing bush larks, which resembled and sang like a skylark, and two species of bee-eaters, beautiful flycatcher-like birds that perched on wires and were tame and easy to observe.

On patrol, I did not carry binoculars; I wanted nothing that might interfere with quick deployment of my rifle, or that might cause serious pain if I fell on them when it was necessary to hit the ground fast. This all but eliminated bird-watching. Thus the only birds I ever identified under those circumstances were either large, like the Brahminy kite, or clearly and distinctly marked, like the rough-crested cuckoo, or slow and tame, like the banded rail.

One of our moves brought us to a forested area—not real jungle, but quite dense and bushy. One of the guard posts was at the edge of this grove, and one eventful afternoon I watched a Philippine coucal use beak and wings and feet to climb up on dense shrubbery. A tiny pygmy woodpecker, much like our downy, worked on the loose bark of a small tree, almost at eye level, and to put the frosting on the cake, a properly named elegant titmouse, which resembled a chickadee colored like a warbler, fed on small insects and paid little attention to me.

Another change of scene found me perched at the top of a steep mountain, from which I watched pygmy swiftlets and fork-tailed swifts flying about below me. Since I was at their level, it made for a novel look at this kind of bird, usually only seen far overhead.

As the war wound down, we were put into garrison at the village of Antipolo. Here we were to regroup, train recently arrived recruits fresh out of high school and basic training, and prepare for the invasion of Japan, in which we were to be in the first wave of the assault on southern Honshu in November. During this period, I got an occasional opportunity for some genuine field work. I borrowed a pair of binoculars, and explored the village for such birds as mosque (striated) swallows, Javanese turtle doves, white-breasted wood swallows and the common mynah, often kept as a pet there as it is here today. A small stream near our encampment led to a sizeable marsh, and in this different habitat I encountered white-collared and river kingfishers, the large and gallinule-like watercock, and several uncertain species of rails and crakes, along with a miscellaneous group of unidentifiable small birds.

All in all, my six months in the Philippines brought me some 35 identified species, and at least twice that number of unidentified ones. My stay there came to an abrupt end, however, when on August 14 the Japanese government agreed to surrender. We were to be spared the assault on the Japanese mainland, but would instead land there as occupation forces. Within a few days of the announcement of surrender, we were on our way.

XIII

Occupying myself while occupying Japan

In Tokyo Bay September 2, 1945, when the Japanese envoys and the various Allied dignitaries signed the surrender documents on the battleship Missouri, our transport ship was anchored just a few hundred yards away. We had been delayed by a typhoon, but had reached Tokyo Bay early that morning and proceeded to our assigned anchorage. At the moment of the signing, we were called on deck and lined up, at attention, though we didn't know why. After the ceremony was completed, an announcement over the loud speakers told us that the surrender documents had been signed and we could stand down.

Early on September 3, we landed on a seaplane ramp at Tateyama, at the end of Tokyo Bay, walking in unopposed instead of under attack by kamikaze planes, artillery and banzai attacks. The regiment was quickly divided into small scattered units, covering the shore of Tokyo Bay from its end to the suburbs of Tokyo. This procedure was a calculated risk, since our small units were vulnerable to attack by any dissident groups, but fortunately such attacks did not occur.

From my viewpoint, it was a great idea, because it got me out into a rural area where there were birds to be seen, and it allowed me to travel around the countryside so that I might get a chance to see them. The problem was that I had no way to identify them. My South Pacific guide was of little use, except for a few very widespread species that occurred all over the area.

After we had been there for a while, one of the men in my squad, rummaging around in a local bookstore, found a small paperback bird book in English, written by a Japanese nobleman named Prince Nobusuke Takatukasa. It had been prepared specifically for tourists and contained beautiful colored plates. It covered only the more common species, those a short-term visitor might be reasonably expected to see, but this, of course, fitted my circumstances to a T. I wasn't precisely a tourist, but I was a temporary visitor with an intense interest in birds and limited opportunity to look for any unusual ones. Virtually every bird I saw well enough to offer hope of identification was there in my little book.

My troop was stationed at and around the big naval air base at Kisarazu, which I understand is now a big commercial airfield. The base bordered on the bay, and had an extensive beach which attracted numerous shore birds, most of which were not covered in my book. Some of the more distinctive ones, such as the little ringed plover and the eastern curlew, almost dead ringers for our semipalmated plover and long-billed curlew, were easy to identify, but the others were just unidentifiable peeps, very interesting but not much help in augmenting a life list.

The airfield also provided me with numerous looks at the black-eared kite, which seemed always to be around, probably looking for prey on the open grassy areas around the runways. Strangely, although we spent a lot of time there, keeping guard on the airport, I never saw any grassland birds. Perhaps the busy airport was too noisy for them, or it may have been because the nesting season was over and they had gone elsewhere for the winter.

The fall and winter seasons were not the most favorable for bird study, but even so I was able to identify about twenty-five additions to my list. Most of them were common birds like the tree sparrow, turtle dove, and grey heron. One day a bull-headed shrike perched on a wire right in front of our troop headquarters, giving me plenty of time to identify it. During a week of posting to a former Japanese base at a village named Futtsu, I recorded an Amur green heron and a Japanese kingfisher.

But birding was not my primary preoccupation in Japan. I was ill much of the time with malaria, and involved with new duties after a promotion to technical sergeant. Our assignment there was to find and gather stores of ammunition and war materiel, store them in a large warehouse, and then destroy them. In my four months there, in a season when there were few of the breeding birds in evidence, I suppose that my list was reasonably good for one who knew nothing about the local birds and had little time to find out.

In December, our regiment was deactivated, men who had recently arrived were re-assigned to other units, and those of us who had accumulated the necessary points were sent home. For a week or so we shivered in freezing tents near Tateyama, waiting for a transport ship to arrive to take us home. Eventually, early in January, the Army gave the order and we were transported to a port of embarkation. On January 7, we boarded our ship, and I spent my last few hours in Japan sketching some of the hundreds of gulls in Tokyo Bay. In the end, I was able to identify only the black-headed and black-tailed, the two most common species and quite possibly the only ones present at the time.

Our ship was one of those liberty ships which had made Henry Kaiser rich and famous, and thousands of soldiers seasick. It was a very rough passage, but I was lucky enough to be given the post of sergeant of the guard (there's something to be said for having a name that begins with a letter early in the alphabet). This gave me the privilege of being on deck at any hour, so I did not have to tolerate the nearly intolerable stuffiness of the holds, where men were stacked in as closely as possible, and many of them were seasick.

At night, standing on deck and watching as the mast seemed to almost touch the water when the ship rolled, I kept thinking of those stories about liberty ships breaking up in rough seas, and thinking how ironic it would be to survive the perils of war and then perish on the way home. Fortunately our ship held together, and on February 3 we anchored in the harbor at Seattle. On February 7, at Fort Dix, New Jersey, I began a new phase of my life as a discharged veteran, ready to return to civilian life and try to pick up the threads of my pre-war pursuits which had been put on hold for four years.

XIV

My Brief Professional Career
as an Ornithologist

My return in February was just too late for me to enroll at Cornell for the spring term, which was perhaps just as well. I still suffered from an occasional malaria attack, and was rather run down and strung out. By not re-entering college until fall, I had time to re-group and once more get into the feel of being a civilian.

I returned to my old curriculum and my old haunts in Fernow Hall in September of 1946, having secured a steady girl friend during the summer. Getting back to the student life was hard, but I was supported by the GI bill and no longer had to put in long hours of work just to keep alive, so I was able to do well academically for those last two years. I graduated in January, 1948, by which time I was married. Marge had a teaching job in the Ithaca schools, and I immediately enrolled for the M. S. program in ornithology, and a year later I received the degree and was cast forth into a very weak job market and with no clear idea of what kind of job I might find.

Through a series of coincidences which would be written off by any producer of fiction as too improbable to be considered, I secured a position for the fall of that year, as an assistant professor of biology at the then New York State College for Teachers in Albany. Through several more unlikely events, I found work for the summer as a junior wildlife biologist at the U.S. Fish and Wildlife research refuge at Patuxent, Maryland. Not knowing what the job might involve, we loaded up our car and headed south.

When I reported for duty, I was informed that the job would start with conducting a bird census in several habitats on or near the refuge. I had never done this, of course, except for the ruffed grouse census on Connecticut Hill near Ithaca, and that census was based on flushing the birds. Now I was to census by sound as well as sight.

The procedure consisted of walking a predetermined route, stopping every hundred yards for a specific period of time. At each stop, I had to identify all the birds I heard or saw, and mark their location on a map. Since there were some local birds in Maryland that I had never seen or heard, I was at first accompanied by someone who had done the census for a long time, but after that I was on my own.

A problem in addition to my unfamiliarity with the local birds was the fact that my hearing had been slightly impaired by explosions while I was in the Army, so there were some birds that I could hear only if they were very close. Still, the work was enjoyable, even if it did involve getting up at four a.m. every morning. I soon learned to distinguish such songs as the very similar ones of the Kentucky warbler and the Carolina wren, the wiry notes of the blue-gray gnatcatcher, and a few others that I had never heard.

What would have happened when the breeding season ended, I don't know. After a couple of weeks, my boss, Joe

Linduska, called me in and asked me if I would be willing to take over a project in Princeton, New Jersey, where I would be working alone. The project was a study to determine the effects on birds of a DDT spray program designed to control the beetles that carried Dutch elm disease. Princeton was full of elms as well as beetles, so it was a good place for a pilot study.

So we packed up again and headed for that old and storied university town in New Jersey. As a Cornellian, I had been taught the song, "Don't send my boy to Harvard," of which the penultimate line was "But send my boy to Princeton, or better far, Cornell." This sounded relatively favorable, but otherwise I knew nothing about the place. We found a small and almost unfurnished basement apartment, not far from the University, and I began to try to get a handle on the research that was expected of me.

It was a daunting task for a young man without prior research experience. I talked with the crew who were spraying the trees, I talked with the property owners whose trees were being sprayed, and most important of all, I looked for two comparable areas, one to be sprayed, the other far enough from the sprayed area to receive no DDT. I would then census the areas and try to determine if the DDT was having an adverse effect on the bird population of the sprayed area.

Having chosen these areas, and received the permission of those on whose property I would have to trespass to search for nests, I set up a schedule. Every morning, sometimes with Marge's assistance, I counted the birds on one of the areas, alternating them so that, in a couple of months, I would have twenty-five or so censuses of each area. In the afternoon, we usually worked together searching for dead birds, or for bird nests. We had made an arrangement with a local freezer locker to receive any dead birds or other vertebrates we found and to keep them until they could be delivered to Patuxent for analysis.

The summer had some non-ornithological events. I worked regularly near the Institute for Advanced Studies where Albert Einstein was employed, and one morning he walked past me on his way to the Institute. One Sunday we managed a trip to the Jersey Shore, and often after work we spent our evening at a local swimming pool, since our apartment was unbearably hot and humid. We were too poor for any recreation that cost much, but we were busy and happy, Marge was pregnant but not far advanced, and we had a good summer. By mid-August, we had accumulated the data we needed, so we returned to Patuxent where, under the guidance of Joe Linduska, I wrote up my report.

A couple of years later, I wrote it up again, in less detail and with more scientific precision. It was published in the Journal of Wildlife Management under the title, "Effects on birds of DDT used in the control of Dutch elm disease." It was my first major publication and one which was widely read and cited for a long time. It was still some years before the long-range effects of DDT began to become apparent, and I played no part in the research that led to that discovery. For my doctoral research, I abandoned ornithology for a thesis on mammals, and for the rest of my professional life I spent my time doing research on fleas, so that summer in Princeton marked the beginning and the end of my career in ornithological research. It did not, however, end my interest in birding, as the following pages will testify.

XV

Birding the Bolivar Peninsula

I n selecting days of especial ornithological splendor, I am led to skip forward some eight years, to the summer of 1957. I had secured a summer school position at Stephen F. Austin State College in Nacagdoches, Texas, where I would teach the general zoology course, field biology and ornithology. My time in Camp Hood had given me some familiarity with the flora and fauna of central Texas, but Nacagdoches is in an entirely different habitat, more closely allied to Louisiana than to the southwest. I knew that I would have much to learn, and eagerly anticipated the opportunity to see new places, new birds, new plants and a whole variety of other creatures.

If I were to rank my best birding days from one to ten, there is no doubt that August 3, 1957, would be included. We had taken the weekend off and traveled to Galveston, intending to spend half of our time at the beach to introduce our children to the ocean, and half of our time birding. We spent the first night at a motel in Pasadena, a few miles north of Galveston, and early on the third we drove to the beach.

There were too many people there to allow for many birds, so we soon moved on to the ferry that carries cars and people across Galveston Bay to the tip of Bolivar Peninsula, a long narrow strip of sand which runs for some twenty miles along the Gulf of Mexico toward Beaumont.

As we crossed the bay, I stood at the front of the ferry watching the many laughing gulls, which people were feeding by tossing bits of bread in the air. I had seen these before, but the occasional royal tern cruising over the water and several black skimmers living up to their name were life birds for me. It was already a good day as far as birding was concerned.

Once off the ferry, we headed up the fine highway which ran up the center of the peninsula. After a mile or so we saw a road of sorts which ran south toward the Gulf. We drove to the end, and Marge and the boys went wading in the warm ocean while I walked up the beach looking for birds. A few brown pelicans soared overhead, but the beach near where people were bathing was empty except for a couple of dunlins.

I pressed on, and was soon rewarded by a snowy plover and a spectacular long-billed curlew, both life birds. The curlew was much like the ones I had seen on Tokyo Bay, but a distinct species. The snowy plover was a comparative rarity, and I have never seen another.

Back to the car, but when we turned around to leave we found that we were stuck in the sand. Luckily, with a bit of careful rocking back and forth, we got out without having to call a tow truck. We drove up the highway, passing corrals where cowboys were moving herds of beef cattle around, but there appeared to be no interesting birds around.

By that time, it was getting on toward noon, so when we came to a roadside picnic table, we stopped and set out our sandwiches and drinks. To my delight, a pair of scissor-tailed flycatchers had built a nest almost over our picnic table, and while they were not as happy with our presence as I was with theirs, they flitted around as we ate. Then we left them to their own devices, packed up and started back to spend the afternoon at the beach. I was happy with my day's list of four life birds and four others new for my annual list.

As we bowled along through a huge marshy area, Marge suddenly said "Stop! There are a lot of egrets over there." I pulled to the side of the road and backed up to where we could see, on our left, an aggregation of birds some hundred yards off. Once again, my "spotter" had come through. In addition to the common egrets and some little blue herons, two roseate spoonbills were feeding in the open water, along with a flock of twenty or so willets.

We were about to move on when a car drove up from the opposite direction and a man with binoculars got out and asked me what I was watching. He was a local birder named John Galley, and I was pointing out the various birds when he said, "There's a pair of black-necked stilts". In another moment he had spotted a snowy egret which I had missed, and as he continued to scan the flock he said "Wait! There's a Louisiana heron." This beautiful bird, which we now know as the tricolored heron, was my eighth life bird of the day.

Except for a day in England and a few occasions in New Guinea and Luzon when I saw a lot of birds I couldn't name, I don't believe that I ever in my life have seen four new life birds in less than ten minutes, and eight in one day. That day on the Bolivar Peninsula remains in my memory as one of the finest birding days in a long lifetime of chasing birds around the world.

XVI

British Birding

We moved from Albany to Fredonia in 1962, and I continued my studies of host-finding in fleas. Early in 1964 I received a letter from Miriam Rothschild, who had long been interested in the same subject. She suggested that I apply for a place on the program of the International Congress of Entomology, which was to be held in London in July, where I could report on my research to the widest possible audience.

This all sounded pretty grand for a poor farm boy from upstate New York, and it required a lot of decisions and some rapid inquiries into funding possibilities. The first step was to get a place on the program, and fortunately the organizers were efficient and that step was quickly taken. The next step, funding, was more difficult. I could not possibly afford to cover the cost of an airplane ticket, a hotel room and food, and other incidental expenses which the trip would require.

The two State University of New York entities that might help me were the new Atmospheric Sciences Research Center at Albany, and the Research Foundation, from which I had received a small grant to initiate the research. I knew the heads of both organizations, and in a short time Dave Barry of the ASRC had promised enough to cover my plane flight, and Mort Grant of the Research Foundation came up with another $300, to help cover other expenses. It looked as though I was going to experience my first plane flight—all that military travel had been by land and by sea—and my first view of the British Isles.

A little before midnight on July 11, I flew out of New York on a TWA jet. It was a very rough flight for the first hour or so, but since I had never flown, I was unaware that this was at all unusual. We flew into a thunderstorm over New England, but once we had cleared that it was a lovely flight, and we landed at Heathrow at 9:30 AM. I took the airport bus to the hotel in Kensington, crashed for a few hours, ate dinner and crashed again.

Since my paper did not come up for a couple of days, I telephoned my correspondent, Harry Hopkins, at the Tring Museum, where the Rothschild Collection of Fleas was then housed. Hopkins was the curator, and I had corresponded with him for a dozen years, sent him a lot of flea specimens, and was on very friendly terms with him even though we had never met. Hopkins gave me directions to Tring, the mecca of all flea students at that time. There I was to meet him, tour the museum, and go to lunch with him. Hopkins told me where to catch the bus, where to get off, and how to get to the museum from there. He greeted me warmly and gave me a tour of the premises. Then he informed me that he was going to take me to his home for "a good English lunch," he and his wife would then give me a quick tour of the countryside, and he would deliver me to the British Trust for Ornithology, which happened to be right in Tring.

He had arranged for an ornithologist to give me a tour of some good birding areas, and this proved to be the first of several momentous days in my birding life to which I alluded in the preceding chapter.

The lunch was indeed all Hopkins had promised, with smoked salmon, peas and potatoes, and hot gooseberry pie for dessert. The tour was short and pleasant, and when he delivered me to the BTO, a young man named Ken Williamson met me. Our first stop was at a place where a very rare and exotic red-backed shrike had been seen. Remarkably, the bird was right there as advertised, and we had ample opportunity to study this handsome bird. A few hundred yards away, Ken paused to show me a bullfinch, more common but equally handsome. Our next step was a marshy area, which at mid-afternoon seemed the most likely place for me to see some birds. In a few minutes I had added seven more life birds, including the impressive great crested grebe, the Old World version of the coot, the reed warbler and the reed bunting.

Ken dropped me at the bus station, and I headed back to London, highly satisfied. I had met and had lunch with the world's greatest authority on fleas, and added a dozen or so birds to my life list—quite an accomplishment for one day.

The rest of my time in London was taken up with the conference, where I delivered my paper to an attentive audience, met Miriam Rothschild for the first time, as well as other flea people, and headed home with a feeling of great satisfaction.

Marge, of course, had not accompanied me, so when in 1977 I got another chance to go to England, this time for the First International Conference on Fleas, we quickly made the necessary arrangements. Housing and food would not cost much, since we would be able to stay in a cottage on the Rothschild estate for a small cost, and eat in the pub practically next door. During the days when I was not actively involved in the conference, Miriam had arranged for bus tours to interesting natural areas, including the East Anglia fens, which promised a chance for more good British birding, and a jump in my life list.

The flea people were a well-rounded bunch, several of whom were interested in birds and helped me with identification when necessary.

Foremost among these was Bob George, another correspondent I was meeting for the first time. My British list and my life list skyrocketed over the next four days. I recorded forty species, of which exactly half were new to me. A few of the others were widespread Eurasian species that I had seen in Japan; others I had seen on my first trip to England in 1964. I saw the coal tit, blue tit and long-tailed tit, flocks of lapwings, song thrush and mistle thrush, jackdaw and hooded crow, green woodpecker, blackcap, and a lot of others. At last I got to see the true robin which Harry Hopkins had promised me but failed to produce.

After the conference we returned to London and took a bus tour of southern Scotland, and at last on June 30 we headed for home, pretty well worn out and pretty well broke, too, but feeling that it had certainly been worth it.

XVII

A Miraculous Day at Presque Isle

I was now well settled in the rapidly growing small college at Fredonia, a distance of only a little over 300 miles from Albany—but worlds apart in every way but mileage. From a sizeable city and the state capital, we moved to a town of no more than 5,000 residents, not counting the college students, and from a growing new university center of some 6000 students to a growing but still small college of fewer than 2000. At Albany, I had largely taught field courses—field biology, ornithology, entomology, conservation, and many graduate courses. In Fredonia I would have to develop a new two-semester course in general zoology, an introductory course in biology, and no field courses—they were the province of the department chairman, Willard Stanley. Stan, as he was known to all, had been in Fredonia for some twenty-five years, had developed the field courses by himself, and was not about to give them up. I was not to get my chance at them until Stan retired in 1970.

This did not stop me from birding, however, and with Dick Miga, who taught at the campus school, I soon became familiar with both the best bird areas and the ways in which birds west of the Appalachians differed from those east of that chain.

In the spring of 1963, however, I got an unexpected opportunity. One of the field trips Dr. Stanley always led was a weekend trip to western Pennsylvania. On Saturday the class would go to Presque Isle State Park in Erie, and then on to Pymatuning National Wildlife Refuge. They would spend the night there, bird on Sunday, and return to Fredonia.

A few days before that, however, Stan came down with mumps, which at his age can be comparatively serious. Dick and I were pressed into service. I would lead the Saturday trip to Presque Isle, then Dick would meet us there and shepherd his charges on to Pymatuning while I returned home.

The morning of May 11 dawned cold and dark, and with a hard frost; about as unpromising a May morning as one could imagine. Still, we were stuck with it, so we left Fredonia at six a.m., and a little more than an hour later arrived at Presque Isle.

We made our first stop beside a small pond, which, though I was not familiar with the area, looked promising. As we started to unload, I saw a very cold and puffed-up warbler perched in a bush. A quick look through my binoculars and I knew we had a good one, a prairie warbler. "Look quick," I told the students as they debarked. "That's the best bird you'll see all day."

Seldom in a life filled with mistakes have I been more wrong. The early morning frost had chilled or killed thousands of insects, which had fallen to the ground. Birds that normally fed in the treetops could find no food up there, and were coming to earth to find their prey. On the ground beside the pond we saw a cerulean warbler, the first and still the only time I ever looked at one from above. Scarlet tanagers were feeding on the ground along with sparrows. On a muddy spot near the pond we saw a dozen or so Lincoln's sparrows, which if seen at all was likely to be a lone bird.

One of the advantages of the frosty morning was that most birds were so preoccupied with getting food that we could watch them without causing them any apparent concern. At close range, we saw a Virginia rail, usually hard to find in its marshy hiding place; a flock of rusty blackbirds, never rare but still not easy to observe so closely; a grasshopper sparrow; and a black tern flying back and forth over the marsh. I suppose that I was the only one on that trip who fully appreciated the miracle we had seen. I know that some of the students developed a lasting interest in birds, and I would like to think that that day's experience was at least a small factor in their choice of birding as a lifetime hobby.

XVIII

My Own Century Run

In 1946, when I returned to Cornell after military service, I tried to take up where I had left off four years before (not easy, since I had taken all of the introductory courses in my first two years and now had to take advanced work which presumed that I remembered what I had learned earlier). One thing I had not forgotten was my interest in birds and birding, and it was with enthusiasm that I looked forward to that year's century run. By the time it came around, Marge and I were engaged, and I was anxious to turn her into the same kind of crazed birder I was. She came down to Ithaca for the weekend, and dutifully arose at four a.m., when I picked her up at her rooming house. She gamely claimed to enjoy it, but she was too level-headed to become a fanatical birder. When, after some sixteen hectic hours of chasing around the Cayuga Lake Basin, she did not call our engagement off, I counted the day a success.

I was anxious to carry on the tradition after I left Cornell, and when I got my first teaching job I regularly took some students out to participate in the Schenectady Bird Club's Century Run. When we moved to Fredonia in 1962, I found no similar tradition except for the Buffalo Ornithological Society's May count, more of a census than a century run. It included Chautauqua county, so I sometimes participated, but it was not the same.

Then, in 1972, a young man in England wrote to ask me if I might have an opening for a graduate student. He had been a student of one of my numerous English correspondents, a man whose interests and writings very closely paralleled mine, and this professor had suggested that the student, Andrew J. Crump, should contact me. As it happened, I was working on a project with a former student, John Baust, then a professor at Geneseo, and after consultation with him I offered young Crump an assistantship working on that research, which involved the life histories of various cold-tolerant insects. He duly appeared for the academic year of 1972—1973, and quickly proved to be an energetic worker. His research on the twelve-spotted ladybird beetle was successful, resulting in a couple of good publications, and he left here in 1974 to pursue a doctorate at the University of London's research station at Ascot.

While he was with us, my other students and I did our best to turn Andy into a birder, but he was somewhat disdainful of what he called "twitchers" and resisted our efforts for a year and a half. A couple of months before he was to return to England, we decided to plan a century run just for him, a last grand effort to make a birder of him. Ken Baker and Bruce Garlapow, my graduate students, loaded poor Andy into the back of my pickup truck at about 4 a.m. on May 16, for a big day of birding.

At 4:15 a.m. we played a tape at the edge of a small marsh (alas, now gone) near Dunkirk and both sora and

Virginia rails responded, the sora flying right by our heads as we stood by the roadside. It was not a really good warbler day, as we had hoped, but we had closeup looks at a fairly rare and fairly spectacular yellow-breasted chat, and later an even more spectacular view of a scarlet tanager. By three p.m., when we gave up the hunt, we were well short of a hundred species, but we had convinced Andy that birding really was fun.

This little story has a sequel: On the third weekend of May, 1975, the participants in the 1974 expedition, with the addition of Rick Bunting, a musician and eager birder, organized the First Annual Andrew J. Crump Memorial Ornithological Foray. The following year the idea was adopted by the Lake Erie Bird Club, and for thirty years the tradition of "Crump Day," a day of totally unscientific social birding, was carried on. It was more casual than other Century Runs, but in most years we recorded our desired hundred species.

Crump Day no longer exists as such, due to a combination of circumstances which are described in the last chapter of this book. It gave rise, however, to a new tradition, which I hope will have as long and honorable an existence as Crump Day has had, and give as much pleasure to as many people, while at the same time giving a modicum of information about the birds of northern Chautauqua county.

XIX

The Day of the Wren Tit

Ever since my brief stint at Fort Ord, I had wanted to return to California, to see if I could find some of the many birds I had missed. In the summer of 1979, our last chick and child having left home, Marge and I decided to treat ourselves to a real summer vacation, which included a week or so in California. I decided that the place I was familiar with would make a good starting point, so we flew to San Francisco, rented a car at the airport, and drove south along the coast to Monterey.

My major objective was to tour the 17-mile drive again. I could not, of course, spend any time on the cliffs at Fort Ord, because that was a military base where I no longer had any business. So, on our first morning, we rose early and, in the fog, drove south. We paused at Carmel River Beach, a very small park where friendly Heerman's gulls begged for food and a lone Monterey cypress made a picturesque silhouette against a foggy background.

We then drove to the entrance of 17-mile drive and started around it. By the time we got a few miles along, the fog lifted, and we were able to enjoy the ocean view, the harbor seal basking on a rock and waving his flipper as though in greeting to the tourists on shore, and the occasional bird. I was disappointed in the few birds. A few cormorants, one surfbird and the normal pelicans and gulls were about the sum total.

We drove on, and a little south of the end of the drive we saw an entry to Point Lobos State Park. You might suppose that this projection into the Pacific Ocean was named for wolves, but in fact it was named for the hordes of sea lions which the early Spanish explorers evidently called sea wolves—not entirely inappropriate, considering the noise they make. I suppose it is possible that the noise might make a nervous fellow think of a wolf pack. For me, Point Lobos will always be remembered as the place where I saw my first and only sea otters and my first and only wren tit.

Point Lobos extends out into the ocean for a couple of miles a short distance south of the Monterey Peninsula. At land's end, you can watch the familiar harbor seals, and also the hundreds of sea lions on rocky islets a few hundred yards offshore. As we stood there, several pigeon guillemots flew by to their nests in the cliffs with food for their young. On the beach black oystercatchers were hunting for food, three species of cormorants and a half dozen species of gulls flew overhead, and a black turnstone lived up to its name, flipping little stones along the ocean's edge.

We explored these ornithological riches for a few minutes, and then it was about time to hit the road. We headed up the path to the parking lot where we had left the car, and a hundred yards away I saw a thick growth of chaparral and small oak trees, which I could not resist. California chaparral has a number of birds all its own. The most common one, the bush tit, is a tiny gregarious gray bird which will remind you of a miniature chickadee, though without the black cap. A flock of a dozen or more will forage through the brush, keeping up a constant chatter of chickadee-like notes, though buzzier and less musical.

Sure enough, I had no sooner approached the dense vegetation than I could hear the tinkling and buzzing as a group of bush tits approached. But hearing and seeing bush tits are quite separate problems. I managed to catch a glimpse of one or two flitting across a small open space, and was staring through my binoculars and delighting in the soft conversations of these tiny birds, which I had last seen at Fort Ord some 35 years before.

A small branch extended horizontally across my "window" and as I watched, a larger bird, very long-tailed and brown instead of gray, hopped up onto the branch and cocked its tail. Its lighter breast with well-defined reddish stripes left no doubt. I was looking at a wren tit, and he (or perhaps she) was looking right back at me from a distance of no more than fifty feet.

Wren tits are among those birds that, like the bush tits, are easily heard but much less easily seen. Deep in the dense cover of the chaparral, they twitter and whistle, but they do not often come up to the tops of the bushes where they can be seen. This one did not stay long; it had enough of looking at me long before I had enough of looking at it, and it dropped back into its cover and disappeared as suddenly as it had come.

Completely satisfied with my day of birding, which had added a half dozen birds to my life list, I headed back to the car and began to pack. I laid my bird book on top of the car, removed my camera and binoculars from around my neck, and prepared to leave. But this day's list of wonders was not yet ended. From the ocean, a hundred yards away and a hundred feet below, I heard a tap-tap-tap like a stone ma-son at work. "Sea otter," I said to Marge, and grabbing my camera I ran for the cliff's edge, Marge close behind.

Below us in the water, a couple of hundred feet offshore, an adult sea otter was lying on its back. With one paw, it was holding a mollusk of some sort on a stone on its chest, and with the other it held another stone with which it was whacking the mollusk. Chips were flying in all directions, and a small otter pup was frisking about, picking up any edible scraps which came its way and crawling up on its mother's chest to get more.

After watching this show for a few minutes, snapping several pictures, we went back to the car, stowed away our gear, and left Point Lobos. There is one down side to this day's story, however. In my excitement at hearing the sea otter, I had dashed away and left my bird book on the top of the car, where it remained as I turned around and left. No doubt some later tourist found it lying along the road, but I could not get along without it, and had to buy a new one at our next stop. This was a small price to pay, though, for a day amid the extraordinary beauty of the central California coast.

XX

The Day I Got the Hat Trick

Rare birds are, by definition, not often seen. I define a rare bird as one that is seen in the area under observation only once in several years, and then usually only one at a time. Every birder always takes to the field hoping to encounter a rare species, and knowing that he is unlikely to do so. A day in which a rare bird is seen is something to be remembered, savored and even possibly boasted about just a little. A day with two or three rare birds is perhaps not quite a once-in-a-lifetime experience, but close to it, and one which the people you want to boast to are going to find hard to believe.

If you are not a hockey fan, I should inform you that the title of this chapter refers to a hockey game in which one participant scores three consecutive goals. It is sufficiently rare to be a big event, and when it occurs and the puck scoots into the net for the third time, the fans who are close enough to the ice toss their hats out onto the playing surface. I'm not sure where this quaint custom originated, but it has given its name to all sorts of similar occurrences.

The equivalent in my case occurred on a winter morning when I recorded three rare birds within a period of less than five minutes. Unfortunately, I was birding alone, so there was no one there to share the triumph with me, or to confirm my incredible good fortune.

For more years than I like to think about, it has been my custom to go birding on January 1, as a good start to the New Year. Usually I will have one or more others with me, but on January 1, 1976, I happened to be alone. At that time of year, the greatest concentration of birds in this area is likely to be at Dunkirk Harbor, so that a trip to the harbor, followed by a trip over some of the local country roads, is likely to produce the maximum number of birds.

Dunkirk Harbor is often a winter waterfowl mecca. A power plant at the west end of the harbor, which uses coal to produce steam to operate the turbines, discharges its excess heated water into the harbor at 85 to 90 degrees, so that the harbor is usually ice-free. Occasionally a northeast wind will blow floating ice in and fill most of the harbor, but on this occasion the inner harbor, at least, was quite free of ice.

Over the more than forty years that I have observed birds there, I have recorded forty species of loons, grebes, swans, geese, ducks and such other aquatic feeders as coot. As is my usual practice, I began at the western end of the harbor, closest to the warm water outlet of the power plant. I had just got out of my car when I saw a loon at the edge of the water a hundred yards or so away. The common loon was at that time (before the outbreak of botulism in the eastern basin) a fairly regular visitor to the harbor in winter, and while they are more likely to be encountered during the migration periods in spring and fall, I was not surprised to see this bird. But as I raised my binoculars, I saw immediately that this was not a common loon. It sat with its slender bill slanting upward, and though I had no other bird nearby to compare it with, it looked to be clearly smaller than a common loon.

I had the first bird of my hat trick—a red-throated loon. This Arctic species is reasonably common in migration on Lake Ontario, but we see one at Dunkirk only occasionally. I was ecstatic to have my first recorded bird of 1976 be such an uncommon one.

Having satisfied myself fully of this bird's identity, I began to scan the west end of the harbor. On the rocks, a sort of barrier to prevent erosion of the power plant property when the wind is in the northeast, I saw a small bird sitting. This is not a likely place for a bird to be sitting, so I took a careful look, and saw at once that it was a purple sandpiper, a bird seen here even less often than a red-throated loon. I had seen one before, on Lake Ontario in the 1940s, and two at Dunkirk in 1962, but on the average I would estimate that we see one here about once in every ten years.

The purple sandpiper is a remarkable bird. Normally it remains along the Atlantic Ocean, but every now and then one gets far enough inland to find open water on one of the Great Lakes. It is likely that some of these are blown in by a storm, though there may be some sort of migratory movement in November, since most records are from that month. Winter individuals are certainly wanderers, either storm-blown or with a poor sense of direction.

I admired the purple sandpiper for a minute or so and then turned my attention to the other side of the small point of land on which I was parked. There, riding along on the calm waters of the harbor, was a small grebe. Horned grebes are not uncommon in the harbor at that time of year, but this bird did not have the snowy white cheeks and neck of the horned grebe. Its grayish neck, coupled with a dark crown that extended below the eye, marked it as an eared grebe, a western species which was first identified in western New York in 1950, and which, since then, has turned up quite a few times. In fact, I had observed the first one I had ever seen from this same point of land a year previously.

My ornithological hat trick was complete, and my birding year was off to a wonderful start. In my birding life, I have had a lot of great days, as some of the other vignettes in this book will tell you, but I have never recorded three such rare species in such a short space of time, and I'm sure I never will again.

XXI

A Continental Diversion

Both Marge and I like to travel, so whenever our finances allowed we tried to see as much of the world as we could. We had seen most of the United States (except Hawaii and Alaska), and by 1990 had toured most of England and Scotland. Our only venture onto the continent had covered parts of the Netherlands, western Germany, Switzerland and France, mostly in a superficial manner, of course, and with a special emphasis on gardens, since the trip took place during the first half of May.

In 1993, we read about a tour called "Country Inns of Europe." Except for a couple of days in Luzerne, Switzerland, it was entirely new ground for us, and being country people ourselves we liked the idea of its emphasis on small towns. I thought it might offer an opportunity to see some new birds, and many of the side trips sounded interesting too. There was a trip to Vienna, one to Salzburg, another to

Luzerne, and we would end up in Geneva, but our hotels were all in small towns or even in the country. It sounded as though it would be right up our alley, and so it proved to be.

We flew to Frankfurt, but our hotel was not in the city but in the small suburb of Mainau. We walked around the village that evening and I saw my first European birds of the year, a blackbird and a carrrion crow, both common species that I had seen before.

The next day we headed southeast, our target being the small medieval town of Dinkelsbuhl. This charming village had to be approached through an imposing city wall, and a sign on the side of our hotel announced that it had been built in the 15th century. We paused that day for lunch at Gotzenburg Castle, build by the famous Gotz Iron-hand, named for a prosthetic device which he had made to replace a hand lost in battle. We not only saw the hand, we also had a look at a very tame and accommodating great tit, my first life bird of the tour. Then as we approached Dinkelsbuhl I was able to identify a sparrow hawk, roughly the European equivalent of our sharp-shin.

We spent two days at Dinkelsbuhl, and then headed south into Austria. We had lunch at the village of Eichstadt, near the famous Solenhofen site where the first fossil bird, the Archaeopteryx, was found. I was tempted by some of the fossils on sale, but opted instead for a walk around the village, where we were rewarded by views of my first European nuthatch.

Our hotel that night was the most rural of all, and it took our driver a long time and several stops for directions to find it. It was located on a small lake called Irrsee, and was surrounded by farms. Walking out of the door, we soon found ourselves surrounded by cow pastures. We spent two nights here, and I spent a lot of time on the balcony of our room overlooking the lake, trying to identify the birds there. Most of them were what my book called Slovenian grebes, but they were just horned grebes to me. In the surrounding farmland, though, I added greenfinch and linnet to my life list.

After two nights there, we were off to Vienna for the day, and then on to the village of Kitzbuhel for the night, where we stayed in an elegant hotel such as might have entertained Emperor Franz Joseph many years ago.

The next day we headed toward Switzerland. With a short stop in Lichtenstein, mostly so we could get souvenirs in a huge gift shop, we entered Switzerland and on to our hotel in the village of Weggis, down Lake Luzerne from the city. On our boat trip into the city the next day, I had good views of a shag, a great crested grebe and numerous ducks.

Back in Weggis that evening, we had coffee on the porch of a small café overlooking the lake. I saw a lot of water birds, but only one, the pochard, was entirely new to me. The next day we were off again, to the remote village of Lenk, surrounded by the high Alps, where we lived it up in a huge suite on the top floor of the hotel. En route, our tour guide had arranged for a stop at a Swiss farm in the area known as Simmental, a lovely valley surrounded by mountains. There the Buehler family, who raised horses and often sold them in the United States, had laid out a spread of local breads, cheeses and wines, and while others ate I prowled in the garden, where there were numerous birds flying around. I saw my second European robin and my second black-cap, and then, in an adjacent field, I saw a small blue-gray bird fly to the top of a pole. There it did a series of bobbing "pushups," exactly in the manner of the American rock wren. I had a good look at the bird, and while I had no idea what it was I was certain that I could find it when I had time to go through the field guide which was in my suitcase.

Sadly, this proved not to be the case. I could not find anything that looked exactly like it, and no mention of that peculiar bobbing. After I arrived home, I got out my directory to the members of the American Ornithologists' Union, looked up the names of members from Switzerland, and selected one at random. I wrote to him with a description of the bird I had seen and asked if he could identify it. By good luck, I had picked a man who had been in the U. S. A., and was familiar with the rock wren. The bobbing behavior, he told me, was distinctive. The bird I had seen was a female black redstart, and this kind gentleman also sent me a paper he had written on birds of the Simmental.

We were nearing the end of our trip, and the only additional life bird I saw was a honey buzzard flying about near Montreux. The next day we flew out of Geneva to Frankfurt and then home. Our country inn trip had lived up to all of our expectations in terms of scenery, historical information, medieval villages and all of the other things we had seen, and in addition I had added ten species to my life list. Ignoring the views of palaces and city walls, the highlights for me were the hotel in a cow pasture on the shore of Irrsee, and an hour in a delightful Swiss garden.

XXII

Companions in Birding

In 65 years of serious birding, I have had, of course, hundreds of field companions—thousands if you count the students I have led on bird trips. Even though I never became a truly professional ornithologist, I never lost my enthusiasm for birding, and the joy of seeing the most beautiful and enchanting of all living organisms.

Most of the time, birding is not a solo activity. It's true that when I was in the Army, I had to bird alone because no one else was interested, but for the most part the companionship is as important as the birding. A good bird trip with agreeable companions can be rewarding even if the birding is lousy, and when two companions share the pleasure of a good birding day the enjoyment is more than doubled.

At Cornell, I had the good fortune to be surrounded by pleasant and knowledgeable birders, who were happy to share their knowledge and their enthusiasm with an ignorant beginner. In those first two years, my fellow birders included many who would make it into the upper echelons of ornithology: Dwain Warner, Bob Mengel, H. B. (Bud) Tordoff, Ed Reilly, Steve Eaton, Ken Parkes, Harold Axtell, Ernest (Buck) Edwards, Sally Foresman, who became Sally Hoyt and later, after the death of her first husband, Sally Spofford.

My closest birding companions during those formative years included one of the above, Harold Axtell; Herb Bleich, a wonderful and witty boy from New York, who was killed in World War II, and Rudd Stone, a wild and crazy guy, one of my best friends. Harold, as noted earlier, had left a career as a musician to become an ornithologist. Once he had at last accomplished that, he spent his career as a curator at the Buffalo Museum of Science. Rudd worked in various museums, most of the time at Holyoke, MA. All three were skilled birders; I learned more from them than from any classes.

Sally Spofford was a good friend for many years. While still at Cornell, she married Southgate Hoyt, a fellow graduate student, who died of cancer while still in his forties. Some years later she married Walter Spofford, noted for his work with raptors, and after their retirement they moved to Portal, Arizona. Here they entertained thousands of birders from all over the world, who came primarily to expand their lists of hummingbirds at the Spofford nectar feeders.

I have been associated with Steve Eaton in many ways since our student years. He became a professor at St. Bonaventure University, only about fifty miles from Fredonia, and we were both active, beginning in the 1950s, in the Federation of New York State Bird Clubs, where Steve served as editor of their journal and I eventually worked my way up to President. In the last twenty years we have both labored with the Roger Tory Peterson Institute in Jamestown, and have had many opportunities to work together.

When I left college and took up teaching duties in Albany, Rudd Stone was at his home in Schenectady. He introduced me to the birders of the Schenectady Bird Club, with whom I enjoyed many happy hours of birding. In particular, Minnie Scotland, my department chairperson and a confirmed birding enthusiast, helped me to learn where to look for birds in my new environment. But one of my closest associates in those years was not in the academic or scientific world, though he was a better scientist than many who had academic credentials. Dan Smiley was one of the proprietors of the legendary Mohonk Mountain House, near New Paltz. We met as members of the Nature Conservancy in the early 1950s, and were fast friends and co-workers in many endeavors until his death. I led Nature Week programs at Mohonk a number of times, and Dan was an enthusiastic participant in my flea research, and co-author of some of my papers, as well as a delightful companion on many field trips.

Since I came to Fredonia more than forty years ago, I have been taught about the local environment by Dr. Willard Stanley, my department chairman for fifteen years and Chautauqua County's authority on local birds. I have shared field experiences with many local birders, but particularly with Dick Miga and Terry Mosher, and until he moved away, Rick Bunting. Best of all, I had the privilege of instructing, for thirty-five years in Albany and Fredonia, young men and women who have found birding to be an important part of their lives, and who have been, for a few years at least, an important part of mine. A few have become professional ornithologists, or have moved into some other field of biology, but others are just interested birders.

I don't suppose that there are any birders of the last half of the 20th Century who would not like to list Roger Tory Peterson as a birding companion. But despite his abounding energy and his wide travels, there are not many left who can make that claim, and I am not one of them. Still, you could not be a birder during this period and ignore the impact on your birding life of this man who has been described as the most influential bird student since John James Audubon.

I first felt his influence in 1940 when, as a beginning student in ornithology, I used the first edition of *A Field Guide to the Birds*. A few years later I used the western guide in my Army-sponsored travels. The man himself, however, remained unknown to me until the mid-1950s.

I finally saw him in person at the annual meeting of the National Audubon Society in New York City in 1955. He was at that time the Director of Education for the Society, so he was on the program as a speaker, and he also led a field trip to the New Jersey shore, in which I participated. Of course I didn't meet him; there was a large multitude of eager birders who surrounded him, so I had to wait some years for a more personal meeting.

That occurred in Schenectady, when he brought an Audubon Screen Tour presentation there, and I was one of the members of the Schenectady Bird Club chosen to join him at dinner. Over the next few years I saw him occasionally at one meeting or another, but I rarely had occasion to speak to him during those years.

My closer association, though, was not with the man himself, but with the institution he founded to carry on his work. From the moment it was announced that he was considering the establishment of the Roger Tory Peterson Institute in Jamestown, I wanted to help realize it in any way possible, and I'm very proud that I was able to be helpful in any number of small ways during the institute's formative years. After some years of preparation, the Institute became a reality, and today plays a major role in the environmental education field.

Throughout my retirement years, Marge and I have been associated with the Institute, which I suppose was the reason I was one of those asked to offer a brief tribute to Peterson at his memorial service in Jamestown. While I never knew him well, I shared with him a deep commitment to nature education, and the belief that once instilled in a young person, love of the natural world is never lost. I have spent my life in promoting these beliefs, and it has been a pleasure to watch the development and growth of the Institute from small beginnings to its present stature.

Last of all, I offer a word of wisdom from an old man to young birders. Cherish your field companions. Birders are by and large pleasant, affable, considerate and liberal in sharing information. Some of them are intensely competitive, and I suppose there are some who are surly and disagreeable, but those who share your joyful days afield will surely leave you with a lifetime of happy memories like those I have tried to share with you in these brief vignettes.

XXIII

An End and a Beginning

As I write this last "big birding day" account, I am approaching my eighty-third birthday. I have just returned from another of those May Century Runs, one exciting enough to be included as this book's final chapter.

I have written in an earlier chapter about the establishment of the Andrew J. Crump Memorial Ornithological Foray, which came to be known to local birders as "Crump Day." Each year, as new members joined our bird club, I had to explain who Crump was and review the circumstances which led to this annual day of fun and social birding.

At the April 2004 meeting of the Lake Erie Bird Club, one member questioned the desirability of having a May big day named for a man whom no one (except me) knew or had ever met. In reality, perhaps he was just sick of hearing my lengthy explanation every year. In any case, he suggested that the club should vote to re-name it for the club's oldest member, and call it the Allen Benton Ornithological Foray.

Although I did not approve, the motion passed, and the date of May 21 was set for the changeover from Crump Day to the Benton Foray. That day has now come and gone, and a brief account of it makes a fitting conclusion to the story of one man's birding through life.

Since the Foray is intended to be a relaxing day of low-pressure birding, we did not meet until seven a.m., by which time the best three hours of the day had passed. To make it worse, the weather report was extremely unfavorable. I woke up at three a.m. to the sound of rain pounding on the roof outside my window. Well, I thought, maybe it will clear up in four hours, though it was indeed a forlorn hope, according to the weather forecast. At four I got up and turned on the television weather station. More bad news: severe thunderstorms were forecast for the entire day, with seemingly very little chance that they would miss us. It seemed that the weather gods did not approve of the Benton Foray any more than I did.

At six, when I again awoke, it was cloudy and damp but at least not raining. I quickly dressed and ate breakfast, and when I left for our rendezvous point the sky was fairly bright, though by no means sunny. I was happy just to get the trip started under relatively good conditions, though I had no expectation that we would escape a major storm.

To end the suspense right here, I will tell you that at three p.m., the sun was shining brighter and the first Benton Foray had gone off with no more than an occasional sprinkle. No thunder and lightning, no hail, no gale force winds. The weather station was still reporting severe storms and even a possible tornado, as we sat at home, cozy and dry after a short but entirely pleasant day of birding.

For me, it was a resounding success. We divided into two groups of about ten each, and in the group I joined my companions recorded sixty-three species. The other group had a similar species count, and enough of them were different to allow us to break the desired 100 total; not bad for a day that started at seven a.m. and ended in mid-afternoon.

Of course with less than perfect sight and worse hearing, I did not list all of those sixty-three species, but I saw and heard more warblers than I usually do, and since these little jewels are my favorite birds that alone made the day a success for me. I no longer go out alone into the woodlands where most warblers are recorded, so that means that I can see them only when I am with a group, or when a few species wander through my yard.

May 21 is just a little past the optimum date for migratory birds at our latitude. The early warblers are already gone to the north, while the later Tennessee, blackpoll, and bay-breasted are just arriving. Our list of a dozen warbler species was good for the time of year. Particularly cooperative Wilson's and magnolia warblers flitted about in full view, in spite of the advanced vegetation which effectively concealed many of the birds which others could hear but no one could see.

Another highlight occurred when we paused to see if any waterfowl were using a small farm pond. There were none, but at that moment an osprey came over and paused to check out the same pond, circling low over our heads as though he might be watching us watching him. We knew that he had only fish on his mind, but it was exciting to watch him at such close range. After circling around several times, he apparently concluded that the pond was as useless for his purpose as it was for ours and wandered off.

You may wonder why an osprey, which is pretty common, should be so interesting. For the past two or three years, there have been persistent rumors of a pair of ospreys nesting near the place where we saw this one, and May 21 is well past the usual migratory period for the species. Perhaps this will be the year when breeding will be confirmed, just in time to be included in the second state-wide survey of breeding birds, now in its fifth and final year.

Other species which will not seem particularly interesting to you, but which I enjoyed because I seldom see them any more, were a foraging blue-gray gnatcatcher, a singing male indigo bunting, and a black-billed cuckoo, with a voice so loud that even I could hear it. At about ten thirty a.m., I gave up the pursuit, feeling that I had walked about enough for one day, and went home pleasantly surfeited with birding delights.

I hope that the First Annual Benton Foray will not be my last, but even if it is, I'm sure that many of the local birders will carry it on. Sometime in the future, some club member will ask, "Why do we have to call our May big day after someone no one here ever knew or even met?" and the name will change again. In the meantime, I hope the participants will derive as much pleasure and satisfaction from the foray's activities as I did from this first one.

And last of all, I hope you have enjoyed this journey through a birder's life as much as I have enjoyed re-living it in these pages.

Afterword: Meghan's Page

He walks through the marshy land, eyes open for frogs and bugs, ears perked to the calls of birds. The camera hangs heavy around his neck, telephoto lens ready to capture the grace of a butterfly, or the striking crimson of holly berries against dull brown branches. He points these things out to me from behind the camera, crouching to find the perfect angle, snapping the lens and claiming another piece of a fall day for his own.

These are the lessons of my grandfather. Instead of buying me toys he led me on walks through the woods, teaching me the calls of bluejays, cardinals, and finches. We discovered spiders' webs stretched from weed to weed, and watched as thousands of tiny praying mantises found their way into the world. His life experiences became my lessons, and now as he turns eighty and I turn eighteen, I am beginning to realize how valuable those lessons truly are.

Allen Benton has been many things. He has been a farmer, a soldier, and a teacher. He has written poetry, a newspaper column, and biology textbooks. He has traveled the world, been a colleague of famous naturalists, and won photography contests. Yet to me. he is the soft-spoken humble man who held me on his knee and sang "O Clementine" when I was a child, and taught his grandchildren how to find the best raspberries. He is my Gramps, who puts mousse in his hair and does crosswords curled on the couch, tennis shoes left haphazardly on the floor.

I find parts of him in myself when I hold a camera or write a poem. My love and respect for nature mirror his own, and I dream of accomplishing as many things in my life as he has. I don't want to be confined to one thing, one future, and he has taught me that you can do everything you want to do, with a little determination and drive. His Christmas gifts to me have been books: volumes of Whitman, old copies of *Anna Karenina*. Those are things I will cherish long after I have outgrown sweaters and dolls.

Someday I will teach my children how to find the perfect raspberry, reddened and ripe. I will show them spiders and teach them the voices of birds. They will know they are part of something much bigger than themselves, as I was taught to know, and carry with them into adulthood a sense of duty to the world.

—Meghan Rutherford